Playtime

Lunchtime

Bathtime

Bedtime

How you can help

Understanding the concept of time and learning to tell the time are big steps in any child's life. **First Steps** *time* looks at the idea of time, using appealing illustrations to tell the story of a brother and sister's day, from getting up in the morning to going to bed at night. Each of the familiar scenes is related to the time on a clock face.

 Enjoy talking about the illustrations together. What is Sally doing in this picture? What do you do first in the morning – eat breakfast or get dressed? The little mouse echoes the actions and provides lots of opportunities for talking and laughing.

There are lots of other ways you can help your child learn about time. Look for different clocks at home or outdoors. Enjoy talking about the day's events, using ideas like before, after, etc. Counting rhymes, songs and games like "What Time Is It, Mr. Wolf?" will help, too.

*To avoid the clumsy "he/she",
the child is referred to throughout as "he".

Ladybird would like to thank Priscilla Hannaford, freelance editor on this series.

Published by Ladybird Books Ltd.
27 Wrights Lane London U.K.
A Penguin Company
© LADYBIRD BOOKS LTD. 1997
LADYBIRD and the device of a Ladybird are trademarks of Ladybird Books Ltd.

time

by Lesley Clark
illustrated by Peter Stevenson

Ladybird

It's 7 o'clock.

GOOD MORNING!

It's daytime, and Sally and
Billy are wide awake.

What do they do first?

Talk with your child about the order in which he does things in the morning. What does he do first?

It's 8 o'clock.

They get washed.

I'm quick
at washing...

What things can your child do quickly? What things does he do a little more slowly?

It's 9 o'clock.

What do Billy and Sally do *next*?

It's 10 o'clock.

What do *you* do in
the mornings?

It's 11 o'clock.

Sally is having a drink.

It's 12 o'clock and it's the middle of the day.

It takes a long time to get it ready but a short time to eat it!

It's 1 o'clock.

GOOD AFTERNOON!

Billy and Carla are having a race.

My bike is slow.

My car is fast.

It's 2 o'clock.

Billy helps Mom hang
the laundry out to dry.

What do you do in the afternoon?

Look at the time!
It's 3 o'clock.

Time to pick Sally up from school.

Talk about how clocks are useful for reminding us when to do something and how much time we have to do it.

It's 4 o'clock.

Look at the pictures of
Sally and Billy baking a cake.

What do they do first?

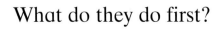

It's 5 o'clock.

GOOD EVENING!

It's getting late.

Everyone is hungry.

Who's already got an empty plate?

It's 6 o'clock.

It's bathtime.

I've had my bath. I'm ready for bed.

Now it's Sally's turn to take a bath.

It's 7 o'clock.

It's nighttime.

Time for Sally to go to bed.

Come on Sleepyhead, it's time to say your prayers.

At night it's dark.

What things happen while you're asleep?

Talk about what happens in your child's night and day.

Look at clocks throughout the day.
When do you eat, bathe and play?

7 o'clock

8 o'clock

9 o'clock

2 o'clock

3 o'clock

4 o'clock

10 o'clock   11 o'clock   12 o'clock   1 o'clock

5 o'clock   6 o'clock   7 o'clock

What a busy week!

On Monday Billy goes to preschool.

On Tuesday he stays with Grandma.

On Wednesday Carla comes to play.

On Thursday Billy goes shopping.

On Friday Billy and Carla go swimming.

On Saturday Billy plays with Sally.

And on Sunday he goes to church.

Keep a weekly record of regular activities, and paint or cut out pictures to help your child remember the sequence.

First Steps

Aimed at children aged 2 and up, the mini hardback books in the **First Steps** series are designed to complement one another and can be used in any order.

mini hardbacks

- abc
- 123
- colors and shapes
- sorting and opposites
- time

Durable hardback books use photographs and illustrations to introduce important early-learning concepts.

from **First Steps** *abc*